Majestic
Mountains

Written by Anna Porter
Series Consultant: Linda Hoyt

WorldWise™
Content-based Learning

Contents

Introduction

Mountains are the tallest landform on Earth. They rise high above the surrounding land, and their peaks are often covered with snow.

Many animals, birds and even people live on mountains – but these beautiful, majestic landforms can also be dangerous places for all who live on them.

5

Chapter 1

How are mountains formed?

Mountains are formed on land or on the ocean floor when parts of the earth's surface are pushed upwards. This usually happens very slowly, over millions of years.

Mountains formed from inside the earth's crust

Some mountains are formed when two rocky **plates** in the earth's crust crash against one another. The land bends, **buckles** and rises up in different shapes. These shapes make a line of mountains called a mountain range. Mountain ranges form slowly over millions of years.

The Andes Mountains are found in several countries of South America and make up the longest range in the world. It is 7,500 kilometres long.

The Himalayan mountain range forms the great mountain system of Asia. It includes Mount Everest – the highest mountain in the world.

Mountains formed from volcanoes

Other mountains are formed from volcanic activity. When a volcano erupts over and over again, **lava** gushes over its side and builds up. The lava then cools and hardens, which makes a mountain. Sometimes, this happens on land – Mount Fuji in Japan was formed this way.

Mount Fuji, Japan

Volcanoes can also erupt and build up from the ocean floor. Their peaks push up above the water's surface and become islands. But most of these mountains are underwater.

Chapter 2

The different parts of a mountain

Most mountains are more than 600 metres high, and some are more than 7,000 metres high. Life at the top of a high mountain is very different from that at the bottom.

At the top

The tops of high mountains are covered with snow and ice all year long. The weather is harsh, with very cold temperatures and blizzards – these are snowstorms with strong winds. The peaks are bare and rocky, and plants cannot grow on them.

Below the high peaks are steep, rocky slopes where some plants grow and some animals can survive. The animals have coats of fur to keep them warm. Giant birds of prey like eagles and falcons **glide** above these slopes and search for food below. People find it very difficult to live in these high places all year long.

Did you know?

Snow leopards live on the highest parts of mountains in Europe and Asia. They use their paws like snowshoes to help them walk on the snow.

On the steep middle slopes

On the steep middle slopes of high mountains, there is still snow in winter, but the temperatures are not as cold as at the top of the mountains.

In the spring and summer, the snow melts and grasses grow quickly. People take animals, such as sheep and cattle, to the middle slopes, where they eat the grasses. These people stay on the slopes to watch over their animals and camp in tents and small huts. They bring the animals back down the mountain when the weather gets cold.

On the lower slopes

In the lower parts of mountains, there are smaller slopes and **valleys**, and the temperatures are milder. Melted snow that flows down a mountain washes away a lot of soil, but grasses and **alpine** flowers are still able to grow here.

People can easily reach these parts to grow crops such as rice and coffee, as well as corn and other vegetables. Farmers dig out lines of long, shallow, narrow steps in the soil called terraces. They use the terraces to get water to the crops. Making terraces also helps prevent the soil from being washed away down the slope.

Chapter 3

Case study: Mount Kilimanjaro

Mount Kilimanjaro is in Tanzania, Africa. It is one of the world's highest mountains and it is special because it is not part of a mountain range. It is the highest mountain in the world to stand on its own.

This mountain is made up of three very old volcanoes that have not erupted for about 200 years. The mountain's three volcanic peaks are Kibo, Mawenzi and Shira.

Mount Kilimanjaro

At the top

The top of Mount Kilimanjaro is always covered with snow and ice. When some of the ice melts, water flows down the mountain and becomes rivers and streams.

Other parts at the top of the mountain are rocky and dusty places, where plants such as sage grass, moss and **thistles** grow.

Few animals can survive up high on the mountain, but two special animals can be found here.

The white-necked raven

The four-striped grass mouse

15

On the steep middle slopes

Alpine flowering plants and thistles grow in the grasslands on the steep middle slopes. Some birds like to get nectar from plants that grow here. Birds of prey also hunt for food.

Further down the slopes are rainforests, where many different animals live.

Animals that live in the rainforest on Mount Kilimanjaro

Hornbill birds

Sunbirds

Elephants

Monkeys

Leopards

Antelopes

On the lower slopes

Nearly all the rainfall on this mountain falls on the lower slopes, and there is also water from the rivers and streams. The amount of water and the rich soil make the area good for growing crops. People have cleared much of the bushland to grow crops such as bananas, beans and corn. People also grow coffee on these lower slopes.

People visit the mountain to walk on the trekking paths.

Nearly five million native trees have been planted around the base of Mount Kilimanjaro because so much bushland has been cleared.

Conclusion

Mountains are formed in different ways, and they are different sizes and shapes. They are found in many different places – hot, cold or dry places, and even under the ocean.

Many types of animals and birds live on them, and people use mountains to **graze** animals, and to grow and water crops.

Glossary

alpine a plant native to mountain areas

buckles crumples and bends under pressure

glide to move smoothly through the air, without effort

graze to put animals such as cattle in a place where they can feed on grass

lava melted, liquid rock that comes out of a volcano

plates large pieces of the earth's surface

thistles plants with prickly leaves and purple flowers

valleys low, flat land in between two hills or mountains

Index